How to HEAL YOUR BROKEN HEART

Forward by: Apostle Dr. Earl I. Newton, Sr.

RITA J. CARTWRIGHT

KP PUBLISHING COMPANY

ISBN: 978-1-960001-28-3 (Hardcover)
ISBN: 978-1-960001-29-0 (Paperback)
ISBN: 978-1-960001-30-6 (eBook)

Library of Congress Control Number: 2024907823

Editor: Delerice Mackey
Cover Design: Juan Roberts, Creative Lunacy
Literary Director: Sandra Slayton James

Published by:

KP Publishing Company
Publisher of Fiction, Nonfiction & Children's Books
Las Vegas, NV 89117
www.kp-pub.com

Printed in the United States of America

"He heals the brokenhearted and binds up their wounds."

—PSALM 147:3

DEDICATION

This book is dedicated to hurting women who desire
healing from God. No matter what you have gone
through or are going through, you can recover!

God is willing and able to take your pain away.

CONTENTS

Section One
My Unbreakable Path: Triumph Over Heartache

Section Two
Eight Biblical Principles

INTRODUCTION

This book will help individuals heal from life twists, turns, downward spirals, and complete wipeouts. Life experiences are not linear. On the contrary, life experiences come with happiness and heartache. Heartache can lead to a broken heart, which can bring forth many levels of pain, i.e., pain from a break-up, divorce, or loss of a loved one. When a heart is crushed or broken, the aftermath is tragic. Oftentimes, individuals might escape the pain through drinking, drugs, or sex. Individuals may also want to isolate, shut down, or just give up.

Medically, the heart pumps blood around your body and as it beats, it is sending oxygen and nutrients to every part of your body. Biblically, the heart is part of man's spiritual makeup. The heart (spiritual) reflects the real person (Proverbs 27:19).

The heart affects the emotional state of an individual, as well as a person's mind and will (desires). Proverbs 15:13 states,

"A happy heart makes the face cheerful,
but heartache crushes the spirit" (NIV)

Proverbs 17:22 states,
"A cheerful heart is good medicine,
but a crushed spirit dries up the bones" (NIV)

Simply put, when a person is happy, it will reflect inwardly and outwardly. However, when a heart is crushed or experiencing heartache, this can result in a diminished life, an unhappy life.

In this book, I will discuss how to heal your broken heart whether it is from domestic violence, infidelity, and/or loss of your spouse or a loved one. The heart that I'm referring to is your spiritual heart not your physical heart.

While writing this book, my husband, one of my older brothers, and my oldest son passed away. Since their transition, I have been applying the biblical principles that will be discussed in Section Two. These same principles also helped to heal my broken heart caused by domestic violence and infidelity. May God use this book to heal your broken heart, in Jesus' name! Amen.

FOREWORD

Is there a God in this world? Does God exist? If God is real, why did I endure all this heartbreak and pain? If God is real, why won't He punish my abuser? Why can't I get over what happened to me? Many people have these questions in their hearts. Many search for God, yet few know that God exists in our present reality.

You're holding in your hand a life-changing book. This book is an answer to your prayers. Not all books are the same. Some stand out as having made a difference, books that lift your spirit to greater understanding, wisdom, and faith regarding spiritual truth concerning healing. Rita Cartwright's book, How to HEAL YOUR BROKEN HEART, is such a book.

The broken heart is a universal human experience written about, sung about, and pondered over for centuries. It is a pain that cuts deep, leaving us feeling lost, alone, and shattered. But as painful as heartbreak can be, it is also an opportunity for growth, healing, and transformation. Healing a broken heart is not easy, but recovery is possible. It is not only possible but essential if we are to live fully and deeply. Healing from a broken heart is a process that takes time, patience, and self-compassion. We must lean into our pain, face it head-on, and trust that God is with us every step.

I was thrilled when Rita approached me about writing this book. I knew the depth of her own experiences and the wisdom she had gained from her journey of healing and recovery. I am excited about you reading this book because Rita has accepted that her pain is someone else's healing and breakthrough. I know individuals who became so angry with what they were allowed to go through that they refused to channel their anger toward ministry opportunities.

I knew that this book would bring healing to hurting women all over the world. This book would also serve as an open door for many who have felt unable to come out and share their authentic truth. And I knew countless other women could benefit from her insights, practical tools, and compassionate guidance.

Throughout the pages of this book, you will find that she shares valuable personal insights and many practical tools for cultivating a deep and abiding faith in God as you heal from your broken heart. You will discover the power of meditating on healing scriptures for strength, the importance of reading and studying the Word, and the need to protect your ear, eye, and heart gates from negative influences. You will also learn how to process your emotions healthily, and how to find meaning and purpose after heartbreak.

In these pages, you will also find a roadmap for healing from a broken heart grounded in Christian faith and wisdom. If you follow this road map, you will find spiritual success from overcoming a broken heart. You will discover the importance of self-care, self-compassion, and self-discovery as essential components of the healing process. You will learn to embrace your pain and process it healthily while finding hope and joy.

The book is written in a simple and readable style. As you read this book, your heart will be lifted and filled with truths and promises from God that refresh the spirit. I thank God for the blessing of knowing Rita, who happens to be my father's older sister. I have seen and experienced many of the valley and heartbreaking experiences she has overcome. You are reading the written testimony of someone who has gone through what she speaks about. This is more than just a fairytale story. Through all these things yet I see God's leading in her life. I'm here to attest that God's holiness, lovingkindness, and mercy have left an indelible mark on her life.

Through her personal stories, practical advice, and biblical truth, this book is a powerful tool for any woman who has walked through the valley of heartbreak and is seeking a way forward. May you find the courage to lean into your pain, trust in God's unfailing love, and emerge stronger, wiser, and more compassionate from this season than ever before.

Blessings,
APOSTLE DR. EARL I. NEWTON, SR.
SENIOR PASTOR, LIFE CHANGERS GLOBAL MINISTRIES
PHOENIX, ARIZONA

SECTION ONE

My Unbreakable Path: Triumph Over Heartache

Chapter 1

UNINTENDED BEGINNINGS

My stomach was getting bigger and bigger. Although I had missed a few monthly cycles, I thought nothing of it. Being inexperienced with such matters, I thought that since I wasn't having my menstrual cycles that I was swelling up from all of the stuff that wasn't coming out of me. My boyfriend, Jeremy, and I thought we were being careful. But what did we know about being careful. I was 16 years old when I found out that I was pregnant.

We both were raised in the church and lived in a small country town of Randolph, Arizona, approximately 60 miles south of Phoenix. Randolph is a historically African American, unincorporated community in Pinal County. The community began as a segregated town for African Americans from Texas, Oklahoma, and Arkansas to pick cotton in the Gila River Valley during the great migration period from 1930 to 1950. It was formed and named after Epes Randolph, a Caucasian, railroad vice-president. This is where I grew up.

Sex education was not part of the high school curriculum, and such topics were off limits at home. My dad wasn't around. My mom left him when I was two years old. So, I didn't have the advice of my father. Jeremy would try to practice safe sex his way by pulling out, but that obviously didn't work.

My mom had a hunch that I could be pregnant. And it turned out she was right. What surprised me even more was the overwhelming support I received from both my mom and grandmother. They never once brought up the topic of adoption or abortion. However, Jeremy's family had a completely different reaction. His mother sent him off to California, a decision that still leaves me baffled to this day, as I can't fathom the reason behind it.

Before Jeremy went to California, I made the difficult decision to break up with him. Looking back, I'm not entirely sure why I did it. Perhaps it was my way of testing his love for me, but we were just teenagers trying to navigate our emotions. Jeremy pleaded with me not to end our relationship, but eventually he had no choice but to accept my decision. The next thing I knew, he was being sent off to California, and I was left heartbroken, feeling abandoned and utterly confused.

Since we lived in the country, there was plenty of open space to go walking, including a railroad track about 30 feet from our backyard. Across the tracks was plenty of open, uncluttered space. I had too much pride to cry at home in front of anybody; so, I would take long walks so I could cry in private.

Those walks became a ritual: I'd cry and pray, cry and pray, until exhaustion set in. I wasn't even certain what I was praying for, but I knew one thing—I was in pain, and my heart ached profoundly. It was an incredibly sad period in my life. Sixteen years old, pregnant, and alone.

As time passed, the tears became less and less. Then, suddenly, the darkness began to lift, and light began to seep in. The turning point arrived when Germane was born.

One day, Jeremy returned from California and expressed a desire to visit his son. Consumed by youthful pride, stubbornness, and lingering anger, I initially refused to let him take Germane from my house—never stopping to consider what was truly best for our child. So, there we were both tugging at Germane. I won that battle. But soon after, I came to my senses and realized it was essential to allow Jeremy to be a father to his son. That decision shaped the ongoing relationship between Jeremy and our son, one that endures to this day. I had done the right thing for my son's sake.

CHAPTER 2

NAVIGATING RELATIONSHIPS

Two years later, my life took a different turn as I welcomed my second son, Darnel, into the world. However, Jeremy was not Darnel's father. After Germane's birth, I had begun dating a man named Paul. When I first met Paul, he was in the midst of ending a relationship with his girlfriend, Brenda. Unfortunately, Brenda didn't take the breakup well, and she constantly lingered, hoping to rekindle things with Paul.

This awkward situation persisted for about a year and a half. I found it challenging to fully trust Paul during this time. He always insisted that nothing was going on between him and Brenda. Looking back, I realized that I hadn't completely moved on from Jeremy. Despite my feelings, my pride prevented any rekindling of Jeremy and my relationship.

Darnel is here now and by a different man. I felt that I should really try to create a family for my boys, so Paul and I were discussing marriage. In fact, we were hinting at it before Darnel was born. So, we decided to get pregnant because we were planning a future together.

Darnel was born, but our relationship only lasted approximately six more months after his birth. It became clear that Paul, despite his efforts, wasn't the one for me. I made the difficult decision to end the relationship. Paul quickly returned to Brenda, or perhaps he had never really left. Their subsequent marriage was short-lived, as Brenda left him for another man. It was a case of what goes around comes around, and I had made the right decision to leave him. From what I heard, he was quite broken up about it and even started using crack cocaine. It was a wise choice to leave him. Now, I find myself a single mother of two boys, but I've grown stronger through these experiences, and together, we'll overcome any challenge, and we will make it.

I attended a neighborhood party one night, not actively seeking companionship, yet isn't that's how life often surprises us? I've always loved attention from men, which I suppose traces back to my childhood when my father was rarely present. Then I met Eddie. I must admit, he had a certain charm, though his breath left much to be desired, smelling like cheese Doritos. Nevertheless, I decided to explore where this connection might lead, and we began to see each other.

Little did I realize at the time that this would turn into a gigantic mistake.

The first red flag was that Eddie was engaged to my cousin, Kathy. I somehow convinced myself that since Kathy was my third cousin, it didn't really matter. My mom even supported this perspective, and I thought it was rather cool.

Our relationship continued, but the second red flag became evident in the way Eddie's family treated me. They regarded me with contempt, with Eddie's mother unfairly branding me as a whore. Ironically, it was Kathy who was putting on a façade, projecting an image of a goody-two-shoes to Eddie's family. Regardless, I was treated with disdain.

Kathy soon revealed her true colors, and suddenly, my status underwent a transformation. I went from being a perceived whore to almost being invited to sit at the head of the Benson family table. Astonishingly, I chose to overlook all these warning signs, and Eddie and I eventually got married when I was just nineteen years old.

The third and most concerning red flag was Eddie's growing insecurity. He became obsessively jealous of a man named Willie, whom I had recently stopped seeing when I met Eddie at that party. Willie and I had been in love, but there was one significant obstacle— Willie was already married.

Willie and I initially crossed paths at work, and his flirting started innocently enough. However, as time went on, his advances grew more intense, and I found myself drawn into his charm, and it was all good.

Like I previously said, I was raised in church, a Pentecostal church, which is a very strict denomination. I knew it was morally wrong to get involved with a married man, and I resisted with all my strength. Yet, my heart eventually overpowered my rationality, and Willie and I started having an affair.

Our connection deepened to the point where he introduced me to his family, who warmly embraced me. One of Willie's cousins was also his wife's sister, Deborah, with whom I had developed a very close friendship. It became so serious that Willie was contemplating leaving his wife, Sue, to be with me full-time. However, at that juncture, something inside of me snapped, and I came to my senses. Despite our love for each other, I realized I had to let Willie go and allow him to return to Sue, who was equally in love with him.

A CYCLE OF
JEALOUSY
AND ABUSE

When Eddie and I started seeing each other, I still carried residual feelings for Willie, which fueled Eddie's jealousy. Eddie's so-called friends, in a malicious attempt to exacerbate the situation, falsely claimed that while Eddie was at work, Willie would be at our house with me. Eddie chose to believe his friends rather than me, and that's when the abuse began.

He began physically assaulting me, and it escalated over time. Most of the beatings were directed at my face. This was an entirely new and horrifying experience for me. With no father figure around to guide me through such challenges, I felt utterly powerless and helpless. There was one particularly brutal incident where Eddie beat me so severely that even his own mother was furious with him. I was left unrecognizable—two black eyes, a swollen nose and lips, with my entire face severely swollen. It was a nightmarish ordeal. Every time I mustered the courage to leave, Eddie would track me down and forcibly bring me back to the house.

On one fateful night, we had a vicious argument, and I fled to my mom's house, which was also my grandmother's house. My grandmother prayed fervently for God's intervention to change my dire circumstances.

Tim, one of Eddie's closest friends, tragically met his end, a gunshot wound inflicted by one of Tim's cousins, an incident officially declared as an accident. Tim's untimely death left Eddie unable to cope. Nightmares plagued his sleep, haunting visions of his own lifeless body lying in a casket. In a desperate attempt to escape these haunting dreams, Eddie turned to heavy drinking. Regrettably, this only fueled the darkness within him, leading to more frequent and brutal beatings.

One day, while I was spending time with one of Eddie's sisters and he was with his friends, an unusual mix-up occurred; I found myself with both sets of house keys. I went to the house looking for him, and when I discovered he wasn't there, I left with his sister. Then he would come to the house looking for me and leave when he discovered that I wasn't there. This continued all day. During this time, there were no cellphones.

Eddie and his friends decided to venture to Eloy, a nearby town to Coolidge, where we all lived at the time. Both towns, despite their small size, held a longstanding rivalry. Upon reaching Eloy, they stumbled upon a riot between residents of Coolidge and Eloy, triggered by a drug deal gone awry.

Eddie and his friends, mere innocent bystanders, paused to observe the chaotic scene unfolding before them. In the midst of the turmoil, a single bullet was fired into the crowd, tragically finding its way into Eddie's lungs; he died instantly.

Witnesses described the heart-wrenching scene as Eddie struggled to breathe for approximately thirty seconds before succumbing to his injuries.

My grandmother with a heavy heart, uttered, "Lord, that's not what I meant when I said fix it." Be careful what you pray for and be specific.

LESTER'S ARRIVAL: A FATEFUL ENCOUNTER

After the devasting loss of my husband, I found myself trying to put my life back together. I was twenty years old and had already experienced marriage and being a widow after being married for only nine months.

Mrs. Benson in her wisdom, offered me counsel, urging me to embrace my youth and move beyond the shadow of Eddie's death. She said, "Girl you're young, go on with your life. Eddie is gone." I had never experienced such emotional pain before. I look back now, and I believe that the emotional pain was more from shock than from being in love with Eddie. I certainly couldn't love him like I wanted to because of the physical abuse. I decided to take Mrs. Benson's advice and move on in spite of people's opinions. People were saying things like "Eddie is barely cold in the ground, and this 'bitch' is already out on the town."

One day, as I stood in my front yard, two guys on motorcycles rode up. Lester, with his piercing eyes and rugged good looks, immediately captured my attention. He possessed a strong, masculine build and a striking face with a light to medium brown complexion. I remembered hearing about Lester who happened to be from Eloy. I recalled hearing something about his troubled past, including rumors of violence towards women that he was involved with. I'm the type who refuses to pre-judge people based on hearsay. I find out what the person is about for myself.

This was my first mistake—failing to investigate into his history further. My second was being intimate with him on the first day we met.

Lester started visiting me more frequently, eventually leading to the decision that he would move in with me. Soon after, the nightmare of physical abuse began anew. I could not understand why I seemed to attract men with such destructive tendencies. Nevertheless, I persevered, refusing to be labeled as a quitter.

The beatings escalated, reaching a point where Lester accused me of infidelity with my male relatives, barring them from visiting. He extended this control to deny access to Germane and Darnel's fathers, asserting that his role in our family left no room for their biological fathers.

Fear now ruled my life, and I did everything possible to avoid further abuse, even complying with his demands to keep my children's fathers away. However, my compliance did little to protect me from the relentless violence inflicted by Lester.

I worked the evening shift from 2:30 p.m. to 11:00 p.m. at an institution for mentally challenged citizens. One night, after returning home from work, just completing an 8-hour shift and as I walked in the hallway, I noticed a huge hole in the hallway wall. I asked Lester, "How did this hole get here?" Lester explained to me that he had got into a physical fight with Darnel's father who was only attempting to visit his son. I wanted to ask more questions, but I did not want to upset Lester. I accepted the explanation and went to bed.

Later that night I went to wake Darnel up to go to the bathroom. Every night I had to wake him up to go to the bathroom because he was a bed-wetter. I tried to wake Darnel up. He was breathing, but he remained unresponsive. Panic began to take hold as I sensed that something was terribly wrong. My son wasn't waking up. "Lester something is wrong with Darnel; we have to take him to the hospital." We gathered up Germane and Darnel and rushed off to the emergency room in Florence, which was the closest hospital to Coolidge. At the hospital, the attending doctor examined Darnel and told me from his examination that Darnel needed to go to Barrow Neurological Center in Phoenix because he was in a coma.

A coma. I began to repeat what the doctor told me in my head, trying to grasp what was said. "A coma, a COMA!" Again, I asked Lester what was going on with my son.

Lester said that Darnel, who was three years old at the time, fell off the top of my 1972 green Ford Galaxy, which was not working and was parked in the driveway. Apparently, Darnel's head hit the concrete driveway upon his fall. I tried to rationalize what Lester told

15

me because the boys did like playing on my car climbing up and down it. So, this was possible, and plus I wanted to believe him.

The helicopter came to take Darnel to the neurological center. Watching my son's lifeless body on the stretcher through the window of the helicopter was extremely terrifying and heart wrenching. At this point, Darnel was not moving at all. He looked dead.

Upon examining Darnel more thoroughly, the doctors suspected child abuse, directing their accusatory fingers toward me. I could not believe what I was hearing. My son's life hung in the balance, and I was under suspicion for his injuries. The medical professionals claimed that Darnel's injuries were inconsistent with a fall from the top of a car.

I wasn't present when it happened; I was at work. Suspicion naturally fell on Lester and the huge hole in the hallway wall. Lester had no problem taking his aggression out on me all the time. Did Lester beat my son, I thought? Lester was asked verbally this question once again. He insisted that he had nothing to do with Darnel's condition. Because I had love for Lester, I believed him.

All of Lester's family would tell me how much he loved kids, and there was no way he could have done that to my son.

Lester landed a well-paying job in Chandler, a suburb of Phoenix. This new job brought us closer to Darnel, who was still hospitalized. I had hoped that relocating away from Coolidge might reduce the frequency of the beatings, but it turned out to be another unfortunate misjudgment. Through this experience, I've learned that abusive partners often try to isolate their victims from their families, aiming to exert control by keeping them all to themselves.

One day, while Lester and I were downtown Chandler, we got into an argument over something trivial—anything could trigger his anger. Shockingly, he began physically assaulting me right there in public. I felt an overwhelming sense of embarrassment, and I remember a kindhearted Caucasian man shouting, "Stop beating her!" I joined in, pleading for help, praying that I wouldn't be dragged away to face the unknown fate that awaited me once the beatings started.

Lester's jealousy had reached a crippling extreme. In his distorted perspective, every man I encountered or merely glanced at became a supposed affair. It didn't matter if the man was elderly or unattractive; in Lester's eyes, I was involved with them.

Amidst this tumultuous relationship, I also was dealing with the anguish of Darnel's comatose state and the severe accusations of causing his injuries. The doctors had exhausted all medical interventions, leaving my son's fate in the hands of God. They solemnly informed me that even if Darnel survived, he would likely be left in a vegetative state, unable to walk, speak, or care for himself.

In the face of these dire circumstances, I clung to my faith, believing that Darnel would survive and regain his former self. With no one else to rely on but God, I found solace in the doctors who, too, placed their hope in divine intervention. This agonizing ordeal persisted for six long weeks until finally Darnel emerged from the coma. However, the left side of his brain had suffered irreversible damage, leaving him with intellectual disability, the inability to walk or speak, and even signs of blindness.

Darnel was subsequently transferred to a rehabilitation hospital in Tempe, another suburb of Phoenix, where he would spend the next six months on his road to recovery.

Meanwhile, life with Lester didn't get any easier. He would repeatedly point a shotgun in my face threatening to kill me. He would beat me until I was sore all over my body. Then he would force me to have sex with him. He would say to me, "If you ever leave me, I will kill you."

One day, I decided I had to get Germane out of this environment for his sake as well as mine. I don't know where I got the courage to do it, but I did. I moved back to Coolidge to my grandmother's house.

Initially, Lester would visit my grandmother's house, attempting to use his charm to rekindle our relationship. I'll admit, he was an excellent lover. He had the "ship and motion in the ocean." These tactics had proven effective in the past when I attempted to break free from his grip. However, this time, I had an unwavering determination to remove him from my life. He slowly came to realize that this time was unlike any other, as I was resolute in my decision not to return to him.

But Lester wasn't finished . . .

My grandmother's house had a front door with a window in it. One night, the front porch light was off, but I could still see a shadow approaching the front door. It was Lester. I knew from past experiences how his body moves when he was getting ready to beat me. He was rapidly walking towards the front door. I rushed to the rotary phone to call the police, and I barely had three numbers dialed when Lester kicked the front door down.

The local police were aware of the situation. They would say to me, "Call us when he does something." I don't understand this particular law. By then it could be too late.

I couldn't believe what was happening. I didn't think he would violate my grandmother's house like this. Before I realized it, he was pulling me off the phone and was pulling the phone out of the wall.

Lester said, "I have a gun, and I will kill you right here if you don't come with me."

I wasn't going this time! He dragged me though the house toppling over furniture, through the front yard, and through the front gate, which was open. Lester had strategically parked his car next to the open gate. He had the passenger door open and was ready to throw me inside the car.

By this time, I had grabbed the chain link fence that surrounded my grandmother's front yard with my right hand. I am left-handed. Lester tried with all his might to pull me away from that fence, but I held on even with my right hand. My grandmother and mother were praying with all their might. The neighbors came out to see what was going on. I guess all the commotion and prayer caused Lester to give up and leave. I never saw him again.

The next time I heard anything about Lester, he had died. I was called as a character witness in defense of the defendant. The defendant was an upstanding citizen of the community, a family man. I knew his kids. Mr. Smith was not a murderer. He was provoked by Lester. Once again, Lester was behaving insanely jealous about another woman he was involved with. She had kids by Mr. Smith. Of course, Lester's MO was to keep the natural fathers out of the picture.

Mr. Smith was trying to visit his kids when Lester attempted to stop him. One thing led to another. In an attempt to protect himself, Mr. Smith murdered Lester. I told the courts that Mr. Smith had did me a favor. I didn't have to look over my shoulder anymore. Because of my testimony, the charges were dropped.

AGAINST ALL ODDS:
DARNEL'S REMARKABLE RECOVERY AND JOURNEY

Over time, the child abuse allegations were dropped. As I mentioned earlier, Darnel was placed in a rehabilitation hospital in Tempe. He stayed in that facility for six months defying all medical doctors' diagnosis that my son would not live, walk, talk, or feed himself. One day, I received a phone call that Darnel is gaining his eyesight. Months later, Darnel regained his strength to walk, feed, and dress himself with little assistance.

The downside to Darnel's condition is he was diagnosed with an Intellectual Development Disorder (Intellectual Disability). This diagnosis meant Darnel would never live independently. As a result, he must reside in a contained environment. Yes, he is not the same child I gave birth to; however, he is thriving! I'm believing God for a total healing on this side of heaven!

CHAPTER 5

CHARTING A NEW PATH TO HEALING AND SELF-DISCOVERY

W hile residing at my grandmother's house, I felt it was the right time to re-establish my relationship with God. I had come to realize that God was my only source of solace and guidance in my life. My mother and sister-in-law, Charlene, often attended gospel singing programs at various churches; especially, quartet-style gospel musical programs.

One Sunday, my mother and sister-in-law extended an invitation for me to join them at one of these programs. Although I had never attended such an event before, I figured it would be a good way to get out of the house, so I agreed to go.

The performing group that day was called the Angels of Faith. For some reason, I was drawn to the drummer, Randy. The group delivered an exceptional performance, and after the program, we had the opportunity to chat with the members. My mom had her eye on the guitar player, and Charlene had a grin from ear-to-ear, though I couldn't quite discern who had captured her attention.

The following weekend, the Angels of Faith were scheduled to perform in Coolidge, so my mom invited them over for dinner after the program. As I got to know the members better, I continued my efforts to get closer to Randy the drummer.

I started accompanying my mom and Charlene to all these gospel singing programs because, in truth, I had a personal agenda to establish a connection with Randy.

On one occasion, the Angels of Faith were performing at Legend City, an amusement park in Phoenix. By then, we had become quite friendly with the group members and considered them as friends. One of the members, Billy, had a girlfriend, named Mary, with whom I had struck up a close friendship.

It so happened that this particular weekend coincided with my birthday, and I wanted to celebrate it in Phoenix rather than in Coolidge. Mary graciously invited me to spend the weekend with her. After the program, we all went to Mary's house to party; after all, it was my birthday.

Randy had promised me that he would meet me later at Mary's house, but I waited and waited, and he never showed up. In the meantime, another member of the group, Roy, began showing interest in me. Roy, who had never previously displayed any attraction, suddenly appeared quite handsome. Frustrated by what seemed like being stood up by Randy on my birthday, I was taken aback by Roy's advances.

On that night, my celibacy, which had lasted for about a year, came to an end as Roy and I became intimate.

The following day, Roy visited me at Mary's house, and we decided to pursue an ongoing relationship, even though he was currently living with another woman.

Two months down the line, Roy and I made the decision to take our relationship to the next level and move in together. At that point, I was still residing in Coolidge and Roy was living in Phoenix. I wanted to further my education, and Coolidge didn't offer the opportunities I needed to pursue a career and fulfill my education. So, we moved in together in Phoenix.

Prior to us moving in together, one night Roy took me to a gambling establishment on the South side of Phoenix. He looked at me earnestly and asked, "This is the life I lead. Do you think you can handle it?" My answer at the time was a confident, "Of course, I can." Little did I know then just how much turmoil and hardship gambling would bring into our lives in the years that followed.

Once we began living together, a troubling pattern emerged in our relationship. Roy would routinely disappear for the entire weekend, engrossed in the world of gambling. He would leave on a Friday evening, and I would not see him again until late Sunday night or sometimes even Monday morning, just before he had to head off to work. There were occasions when I wouldn't lay eyes on him until he finished his shift on Monday night. It was as if he'd transitioned directly from the streets to the workplace.

As a country girl who had made the leap to city life, I wasn't inclined to just sit at home and wait for Roy's return. I felt lost and overwhelmed. I hadn't anticipated this level of separation and the allure of gambling. I was far from being familiar with the lifestyle he led, and I was starting to realize that I had underestimated the depths of what I had gotten myself into.

Sitting idly at home, waiting for Roy, made me feel foolish. I couldn't help but wonder what he was up to during his extended absences. Our neighbor, O.J., continued to make a move whenever Roy was away. We were familiar faces in the complex, and it seemed like everyone could see how Roy treated me. No one blamed me for whatever decisions I might make.

Roy was becoming increasingly suspicious of O.J.'s intentions, but I resisted O.J.'s advances. Roy, however, couldn't shake his belief that something was going on between O.J. and me, and eventually, he decided to leave.

In the aftermath of Roy's departure, I found myself drawn to O.J. However, it's important to clarify that Roy had misunderstood the situation. O.J. and I hadn't been involved while Roy was still in the picture.

Roy, on the other hand, returned to the woman he had been living with before our relationship began. Despite everything, I was still in love with Roy. We eventually began sneaking around to see each other, and against the odds, found our way back to each other.

CHAPTER 6

MARRIAGE VOWS IN THE SHADOWS OF GAMBLING

Around one year into our life together, my younger brother, Barry, was released from prison. With nowhere else to go, he came to live with us in our small two-bedroom apartment. Living arrangements were already tight since our mother was also living with Roy and me at that time. It was a challenging situation, to say the least.

Roy, being the gracious host, decided to show my brother around Phoenix, which initially seemed like a generous gesture. However, I would come to regret it.

As I mentioned, Roy had a persistent gambling habit, and it often kept him away from home. Now, he had an added excuse to hang out in the streets; he was introducing my brother to the ways of the city; particularly, the gambling scene.

One Saturday night, Roy promised to take me out, and I was thrilled at the prospect of going out. I dressed up and eagerly awaited his return to pick me up. An hour passed, then two, and eventually three hours later, Roy called, but his explanation for not coming was flimsy at best.

I was excited to go out and enjoy the city life, but now I found myself all dressed up with nowhere to go. Stuck at home with no friends in the area, as I had only been living in Phoenix for about a year, and Roy typically ventured out alone due to my discomfort with the gambling shacks. There was no one I could reach out to, and I felt utterly stranded. The combination of hurt and anger I felt at that moment marked a turning point in my life. I was never the same after that experience.

Roy's gambling habits persisted, and it was a constant source of distress for me. There were numerous mornings when I had to head to work, and Roy hadn't returned home from the previous night. I felt foolish, not knowing whether he was alive or not. My mind would race with thoughts of him being with another woman, and he never bothered to call to let me know he was OK. It seemed he had little interest in our well-being—mine and the kids. Once again, I felt like such a fool.

Around two years into our living together, we had a daughter, my third child, and I named her Lolita. It was during this time that I made a vow to myself. When my baby was old enough, I would return to work in order to have at least $2 in my pocket, get my own car, and I was not going to waste anymore nights waiting on Roy. I began to have extramarital affairs.

Despite what was happening in our relationship, Roy and I eventually decided to get married. We got married in Las Vegas. I genuinely tried to remain faithful to Roy because I wanted to, but he made it incredibly challenging. He continued to disappear for entire weekends, and I continued to seek solace in affairs. The pattern of gambling and marital strain persisted throughout the first seven years of our marriage.

Chapter 7

WHEN THE EX-WIFE STEPS IN

R oy and his ex-wife, Renee, had four children during their marriage. When these kids reached their pre-teen years, they expressed a strong desire to reconnect with their father. I wasn't part of the decision-making process; Roy never consulted me about having his children live with us.

At this time, I already had two children of my own, plus our daughter. Given my fair and reasonable nature, I felt that since Roy was helping me take care of my kids, it was only fair for me to support his decision. So, his kids moved in with us. However, this new family dynamic came with its own set of challenges.

Renee and the kids seemed determined to figure out how to push me out of Roy's life. It was a tumultuous journey, because these children were reluctant to listen to or obey me. Thankfully, Roy took a stand and told his kids that I was his wife and needed to be respected.

But one thing remained unchanged—Roy's tendency to spend his weekends away from home, leaving me alone to care for our blended family. I couldn't help but feel isolated and lonely. After all, these kids didn't come to live with me; they came to strengthen their relationship with their father. No matter what I said, Roy wouldn't stay home.

Three of the children lived with us on and off for the next seven to eight years. Initially, they struggled to adapt to our household rules. When they had disagreements with their dad, they'd return to their mom's place. Unfortunately, Renee was often a source of trouble for Roy and me.

There was a time when the kids falsely accused me of mistreating them, which couldn't have been further from the truth. They simply resisted following our house rules, and Renee readily believed their accusations, likely due to her preconceived notions about me.

On one particularly hectic day, I was buried in laundry with about ten loads of clothes scattered across the floor. With six children, one of whom had special needs, plus two adults in the house, the workload was immense. But I always took pride in doing what I had to do and do it to the best I can.

Suddenly, the phone rang, and it was Renee. She told me, "My kids informed me that you've been treating them poorly, like dogs." The conversation escalated from there. Here I was being a mother to her kids, their dad staying out all night long, and dirty clothes everywhere. Of course, I lost it. I always had a bad temper, which is why I established a relationship with Jesus to be delivered from that stronghold.

I said, "Bitch come and get these bad-ass kids, furthermore, you can't come to my house to get them. Call Roy when you get to town, and he will bring them to you." I was so angry I couldn't see straight. I threw the phone through the wall.

Renee did come to get her children at an arranged location. Things seemed fine for a while, but the kids continued to struggle with obeying her. Eventually, they reached out to Roy, asking if they could move back to Phoenix to live with him. While I had reservations, I had no say in the matter. They returned, and over time, we managed to overcome our initial challenges, forming a closer bond. Renee couldn't help but resent that her kids grew to love me as a second mother.

The step kids were all grown up by now and had moved out of our home. Mona, the oldest stepdaughter, had made her home in Phoenix and had gotten involved with a guy and they had a son, Jr.

Renee came to Phoenix, and claimed she was in town to visit her grandson, Jr. Strangely enough, I had no prior knowledge of her visit. Renee had always seemed determined to sabotage our marriage by any means necessary. It was purely by accident that I found out that Roy had met up with Renee in some park while I was at work. He had lied to me about it.

Once again, Roy had shattered my trust in him. The pain of being lied to was the most excruciating. Why was it such a big secret that Renee was in town? That secrecy left me feeling even more suspicious and hurt than ever before.

Chapter 8

STRUGGLES, TEMPTATIONS, AND THE COMMITMENT TO FAMILY

We had two cars now, and I stuck to my promise to myself. Whenever Roy would head out, I would go out, too. Sometimes, I'd go out with my girlfriends, but if they couldn't make it, I wouldn't let that hold me back.

One particular night, I decided to go out alone. Roy claimed he was going fishing, and I couldn't join him because I had an audition earlier in the day. I was actively pursuing a career in acting at that time. So, after the audition, I decided to hit the town.

I had a routine when I went out solo. If I found myself alone at the clubs, I'd sit at the bar. One night, as I sat on a barstool, a very handsome man struck up a conversation with me. His name was

Gerald. I wasn't out looking for an affair, nor was I involved in one at the time. I was simply trying to avoid sitting at home alone.

Our conversation flowed easily, and the night wore on. Gerald was looking even more appealing by the minute. When the club was closing, we continued chatting in the parking lot. Eventually, we decided to sit in my car, and things began to heat up. It was the beginning of yet another extramarital affair.

Gerald and I continued seeing each other whenever we could. He, too, was married and facing challenges in his marriage. Our bond deepened, and he expressed his desire to end his marriage and wanted me to do the same. He proposed getting a house big enough for me and my kids.

Initially, I was swayed by his idea and seriously considered it. But strangely enough, despite my extramarital affairs, I was committed to my marriage and my family. I didn't want to tear my family apart. Roy and I had been through so much together, and I was determined to make it work, even if it meant putting an end to these affairs for the sake of my marriage.

One day, during my lunch break at work, I made a bold decision to reach out to Gerald. My marriage had lost its spark, and although Roy had stopped gambling, he still found reasons to spend time away from me. I would always tell him, "Although I'm married, I feel like the loneliest wife in the world." Tracking down Gerald, who was in the Air Force, proved to be surprisingly straightforward for me, as I've always been resourceful when the need arises. His excitement at hearing from me again was noticeable.

Naturally, we rekindled our connection, and over the course of the next five years, our affair continued discreetly. One fateful evening, as I was celebrating my birthday, I felt an irresistible urge to see Gerald. Roy had taken me out to dinner in honor of my special day, but the longing for Gerald was too strong to ignore. To create a plausible excuse, I enlisted the company of one of my girlfriends, using her presence as a reason to venture out and enjoy a night with my friends.

My girlfriend and I made our way to the Air Force base to meet Gerald and one of his friends. As I was preparing to head over, I found myself short on gas money. When I asked Gerald for assistance, he expressed his inability to provide the funds. In that very moment, a stark realization hit me like a ton of bricks—I had jeopardized my marriage for something that now seemed utterly insignificant. Gerald's unwillingness to even offer gas money served as a stark reminder of how things had changed between us. This event marked the end of our affair, and I never saw him again.

FROM HEARTBREAK TO HEALING: A JOURNEY OF REDEMPTION

ollowing my decision to end things with Gerald, I committed myself to repairing my marriage. Germane had moved out, and Darnel was now living in a group home, leaving my teenage daughter, Lolita, as the only child in the home. Lolita, however, was challenging to handle during this period, often spending time with the wrong crowd and skipping school.

With Darnel in a group home, I made the choice to return to school. I believed that going back to school would set a positive example for Lolita and provide me with the means to achieve financial independence, given my lack of faith in Roy.

One night, Roy and I were hanging out together, still trying to make our marriage work, even if it meant venturing into undesirable places—the 'streets.' On this particular evening, we were looking for some herb to smoke, and one of the women in the group knew someone who could help us. She contacted her cousin, who lived nearby and quickly became our regular supplier. Initially, Roy was the one who reached out to him, but over time, I started contacting him on Roy's behalf.

As this arrangement continued, I struck up a friendship with this supplier, Maurice. It was an innocent connection, and I even attempted to set him up with my girlfriends. When Maurice and I first met, I was still involved with Gerald, and our relationship was strictly platonic.

However, life took an unexpected turn when my father passed away. He was residing in Oklahoma at the time, and Roy, Lolita, and I traveled there for the funeral. During our trip, Roy and I had a heated argument, because of his usual insensitivity causing further distress during a particularly challenging time for me. After the funeral, we made our way to Texas heading to Louisiana for Roy's family reunion. By this point, my anger at Roy had reached a boiling point, prompting me to take a flight back to Phoenix, leaving him and Lolita in Texas.

Back home, I found myself in need of some herb to smoke, so I reached out to Maurice. When he arrived to deliver it, he could sense something was amiss, given our close friendship. Concerned for my well-being, he invited me over to his place for a few cocktails, an offer I accepted in my state of vulnerability. As the evening unfolded, emotions ran high, and lines were crossed. Loneliness, vulnerability, and my anger towards Roy led me down the path of yet another extramarital affair.

About a year after my father's passing, a woman named Lenore made an astonishing claim that sent shockwaves through our marriage and lives; she insisted that her ten-year-old daughter was Roy's child. At this point, we had been together for eighteen years, which meant that Roy had allegedly had an affair with Lenore while we were married. However, Lenore had a reputation for being a pathological liar, which left me in a state of confusion and disbelief.

According to Lenore, she and Roy had been involved off and on for about a decade, Roy admitted to having sexual relations with her but strongly denied a ten-year affair and insisted that the child was not his. I urged him to take a DNA test to determine the truth, but he flatly refused. Lenore was not the type of person to back down easily; she remained steadfast in her claim, even going so far as to inform everyone we knew, including our pastor, that Roy was the father. This relentless situation persisted for approximately a year and a half, casting a dark shadow over our marriage.

Throughout this troubling period, Maurice and I still saw each other sporadically. Whenever I felt like giving my marriage another chance, Maurice would graciously step aside. Despite the mounting pressure from friends and acquaintances, who all urged Roy to take the DNA test, he remained reluctant to do so. I couldn't help but interpret this as a sign of guilt. Still, I desperately wanted to believe Roy. We had invested two decades into our marriage, and despite never feeling entirely fulfilled, I clung to the hope that our relationship could endure.

Finally, after enduring this emotional turmoil for what felt like an eternity, I reached my breaking point. Unable to bear the weight of the situation any longer, I made the difficult decision to ask Roy for a divorce.

At that moment in my life, I was still a college student, juggling my studies with a part-time job. Roy had promised to provide financial support ensuring that our mortgage and car expenses were taken care of. However, as soon as he realized I was determined to move forward with my life, he shattered those promises. He attempted to strip away our home and our only means of transportation—a car that our daughter, Lolita, and I relied upon. The house wasn't just my sanctuary; it was Lolita's too, and our daughter was working part-time to contribute to our household. But Roy's anger and inability to accept the end of our marriage clouded his judgment.

As time went on, Maurice and I had grown incredibly close, and our relationship had evolved beyond friendship. We had already established a connection before my marriage unraveled, so I knew that our bond wasn't merely a rebound situation. My grandmother once wisely told me, "God already knew what you were going to have to go through; therefore, he sent you Maurice." That was over twenty years ago, and Maurice and I are still together. He fulfils my every need, and I have no desire to be with anyone else. I am a one-man woman, but I am no fool. If someone isn't there for me. I won't be there for them. Life has a way of teaching us valuable lessons, guiding us on a path that leads to where we are meant to be.

Chapter 10

HEALING HEARTS: EMBRACING HOPE AND RESTORATION

Now, as I reflect upon the journey that spans 24 years, I can say with certainty that Maurice and I remained devotedly married until fate parted us in the cruelest of ways. Four years ago, Maurice suffered a cardiac arrest, a harrowing moment that altered our lives forever. By the grace of God and the quick response of 911, I became an unwitting instrument of the Holy Spirit, breathing life back into his still heart. His heart faltered again during transport and once more in the emergency room. Sadly, by then, Maurice had endured too long without oxygen and adequate blood flow to his brain, resulting in anoxic brain injury.

He spent three grueling months in the hospital before being relocated to a nursing home for another year and a half. It was in that nursing home that Maurice experienced another, final cardiac arrest, one from which he did not return.

Maurice never made it back home after the paramedics took him away over four years ago. My love for him remains steadfast, and he remains the best husband I've ever had across all three marriages. It has now been three years since his passing, and in reality, I've been alone for over four years. This extended solitude is a new experience for me, but I'm not ready to embrace another relationship or commitment at this stage in my life. I find solace and contentment in my solitude, cherishing my time alone with Father God.

At this juncture, I do not know if I will ever remarry. I will do so only if it is in alignment with God's divine will. My relationship with Abba Father has been instrumental in healing the wounds left by this devastating loss. This loss has drawn me closer to God, deepening my faith and understanding.

In the process of writing this book, ***How to Heal Your Broken Heart***, life presented me with yet another chapter heartbreak. I recently lost one of my older brothers, Tommy, and my eldest son, Germane.

My older brother and I have the same biological father and although we didn't grow up together, we met over 30 years ago, growing as close to each other as though we grew up together. He died exactly eight months to the date after my husband, and five months before my son. In fact, Tommy attended my husband's funeral. I had no idea that would be the last time I would see him alive. We didn't know at the time that he had a very aggressive form of lung cancer. Eight months later, Tommy was gone. He was very supportive of me during my time of loss. If Tommy were still alive when my son passed, he would have been right by my side.

♡ ♡ ♡

Germane was a figure deeply entwined with the very fabric of my being. The umbilical cord that once physically connected us may have been severed long ago, but the bond remained, making his passing feel like a part of myself had withered away.

He and I weathered life's storms together, enduring the thundering journey of domestic violence, his brother's life-altering injuries, his stepfather's gambling and infidelity, and even the dissolution of our marriage. We confronted the heartache of losing my mother, his beloved grandmother, and the grief of saying goodbye to my husband, whom he loved like a dad. Throughout it all, God guided us and blessed me with the gift of fifty-one precious years with my son.

Our children, as I've come to realize are on loan from God. They are entrusted to us, gifts that we must cherish and nurture. In these trying moments, I find solace in gratitude for the half-century of memories and love I shared with my son, knowing that God entrusted him to me to be his earthly guardian.

Germane, like many, wrestled with demons of addiction, succumbing to the grip of meth, and eventually succumbing to meth laced with Fentanyl. But I share this not to dwell on his struggles, but to affirm that he has found deliverance. His spirit has returned to God, where he is now healed and at peace. As the Psalmist David once said, "His son can't come back to him, but one day he can go to his son."

Germane has left behind a beautiful legacy in the form of seven remarkable children plus two bonus children now all grown into adulthood, and most of them even have children of their own. Through them, his spirit lives on, a testament to the enduring power of love and family bonds.

As I continue on this journey of healing; recovering from the profound loss of my mother, husband, brother, and son, I find strength in the embracing of eight steadfast biblical principles, ones that have sustained me and ones I am eager to share with you.

In the forthcoming chapters, I will dig deep into a multitude of healing strategies, addressing the diverse landscapes of heartbreak— be it born from the scars of domestic violence, the shattering betrayal of infidelity, or the profound sorrow of losing cherished loved ones, as I have encountered in my life.

These principles have been my beacon through the darkest nights, their universality and endurance offering solace and hope in times of despair. It is my earnest desire and prayer that through these pages, these very principles may breathe life into your heart, mending its fractures and guiding you towards renewed strength.

Remember, our God is a healer, impartial in His grace. Just as He has mended my heart, He stands ready to mend yours as well, if you open your heart to embrace these principles for healing. In Jesus' name, I pray for us all. Amen!

SECTION TWO

Eight Biblical Principles

FAITH/BELIEVE

What is Faith?

Faith can be defined as a strong belief, trust, or confidence in something or someone, often in the absence of concrete proof or evidence. Biblically, faith refers to a deep and unwavering trust in God and His purposes.

> *"Now faith is the assurance (the confirmation, the title deed)*
> *of the things [we] hope for, being the proof of things [we] do*
> *not see and the conviction of their reality [faith perceiving*
> *as real fact what is not revealed to the senses]."*
> —Hebrews 11:1 Amplified Bible, Classic Edition

Simply put, faith is a belief knowing God will turn anything around; even if, your present situation contradicts your faith.

> *"For we walk by faith, not by sight."*
> —2 Corinthians 5:7 KJV

Why is Faith Important?

1. **Belief in the Unseen:** Faith involves believing in God, His existence, His nature, and His promises, even though we cannot see Him with our physical eyes. It goes beyond what can be proven and relies on a spiritual conviction.

2. **Trust in God's Word:** Faith is closely tied to trusting in the teachings and promises of the Bible. As Christians, we believe that the Bible is the inspired Word of God and, through faith, we trust in its guidance and wisdom.

3. **Salvation:** Faith is essential for salvation. It is through faith in Jesus Christ as Lord and Savior that we believers are forgiven of our sins and reconciled with God. The Bible often emphasizes that salvation is "by grace through faith" (Ephesians 2:8-9).

4. **Relationship with God:** Faith is the foundation of a personal relationship with God. As believers, we trust that God loves us, cares for us, and is actively involved in our lives. This trust fosters a deep and meaningful connection with God.

5. **Strength in Trials:** Faith provides strength and endurance during difficult times. It enables us to

persevere through challenges, knowing that God is with us and has a purpose for our trials (James 1:2-4).

6. **Guidance and Direction:** Faith helps us make decisions and navigate life's complexities. We seek God's guidance and trust that He will direct our paths (Proverbs 3:5-6).

7. **Living Out God's Will:** Faith is instrumental in living out God's will. We trust that obeying God's commands and following His principles will lead to a life that honors Him.

8. **Hope and Assurance:** Faith provides hope for the future. It assures us believers of eternal life with God and a future in His kingdom (John 3:16).

In summary, faith is important because it is the foundational element of the relationship between believers and God. It shapes our beliefs, actions, and attitudes, and it is instrumental in receiving salvation, finding strength in trials, and living a life that aligns with God's purpose and will.

Faith allows us to trust in God's love, goodness, and faithfulness, even when we cannot see Him or fully understand His ways.

"And without faith, it is impossible to please God."

—Hebrews 11:6a NIV

So, then faith cometh by hearing, and hearing by the word of God (Romans 10:17). When you hear God's Word on a regular basis, your faith is strengthened.

Frequently mediating, reading, and studying the Word will also strengthen your faith. This practice will not only build your faith but will help to heal your broken heart. Faith is necessary to believe that Jesus will heal your broken heart. Faith is necessary in order to receive healing from Jesus.

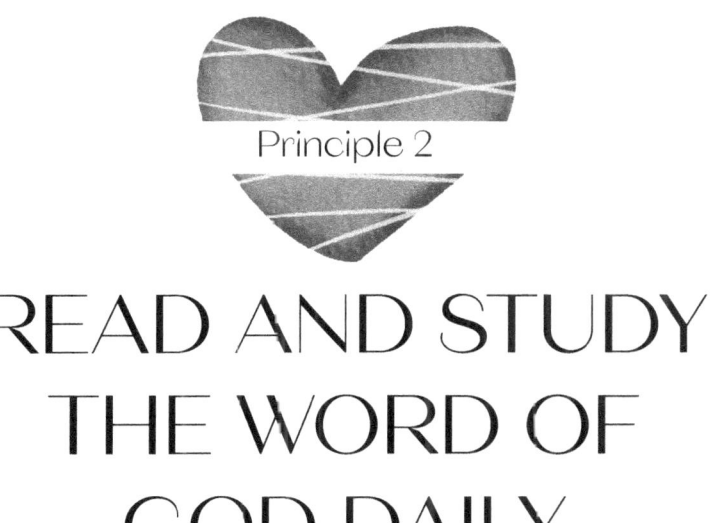

Principle 2

READ AND STUDY THE WORD OF GOD DAILY

Reading and studying the Word of God daily is a fundamental principle in the Christian faith. The Word of God, as described in the Bible, is the sacred and divinely inspired Scripture that contains God's teachings, commands, promises, and the story of His relationship with humanity. It encompasses both the Old Testament and the New Testament.

> *"All Scripture is God-breathed and is useful for teaching, rebuking, correcting, and training in righteousness, so that the servant of God may be thoroughly equipped for every good work."*
>
> —2 TIMOTHY 3:16-17 NIV

"Your word is a lamp for my feet, a light on my path."
—PSALM 119:105 NIV

Jesus answered, "It is written: 'Man shall not live on bread alone, but on every word that comes from the mouth of God.'"
—MATTHEW 4:4 NIV

Why is it Important to Read and Study the Word of God Daily?

1. **Divine Revelation:** The Word of God is God's revelation to humanity. It reveals His character, His will, and His plan for salvation through Jesus Christ. It is the primary source of knowledge about God.

2. **Spiritual Growth:** Regularly reading and studying the Bible fosters spiritual growth. It provides wisdom, guidance, and nourishment for the soul, helping believers mature in their faith.

3. **Guidance:** The Bible serves as a guide for living a righteous and godly life. It offers moral and ethical principles that help you make wise decisions and live in accordance with God's standards.

4. **Comfort and Encouragement:** During times of difficulty or uncertainty, the Word of God provides

comfort and encouragement. It offers hope and reassurance through the promises and stories of God's standards.

5. **Renewal of the Mind:** Studying the Word of God renews the mind and transforms your thinking. It helps you align your thoughts with God's truth and resist conforming to the patterns of the world (Romans 12:2).

6. **Effective Prayer:** Understanding God's Word enhances prayer. It allows you to pray in accordance with God's will and promises, leading to a more effective and meaningful prayer.

7. **Defense Against Temptation:** Jesus Himself used Scripture to resist temptation (Matthew 4:1-11). Regular exposure to the Word equips you to withstand temptations and evil spiritual attacks, which can interfere with the progress of the healing of your broken heart.

8. **Community and Fellowship:** Studying the Bible together with other believers promotes fellowship and mutual encouragement. It allows for shared understanding and discussion of God's truth.

In summary, reading and studying the Word of God daily is crucial for your spiritual journey. It deepens your relationship with God, provides guidance for life, and fosters spiritual growth. It is a source of comfort and strength. Reading and studying the Word of God will help your broken heart to heal.

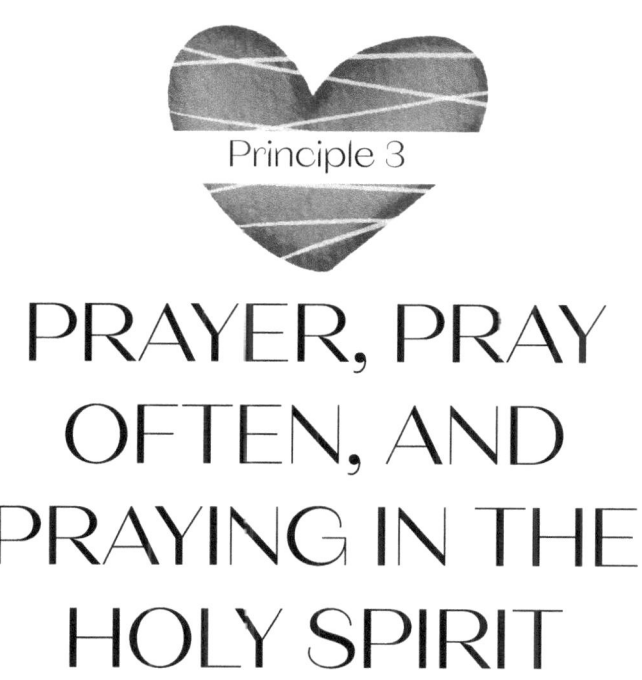

Principle 3

PRAYER, PRAY OFTEN, AND PRAYING IN THE HOLY SPIRIT

What is Prayer?

Prayer is a form of communication and communion with God. It is a fundamental and deeply significant practice. As Christians, we believe in a personal relationship with God through Jesus Christ, and prayer serves as a vital means of nurturing and expressing that relationship.

"This, then is how you should pray:
Our Father in heaven,
* hallowed be your name,*
* your kingdom come,*

your will be done,
  on earth as it is in heaven.
Give us today our daily bread.
And forgive us our debts,
  as we also have forgiven our debtors.
And lead us not into temptation,
  but deliver us from the evil one."

—MATTHEW 6:9-13 NIV

"Do not be anxious about anything, but in every situation, by prayer and petition, with thanksgiving, present your requests to God. And the peace of God, which transcends all understanding, will guard your hearts and your minds in Christ Jesus."

—PHILIPPIANS 4:6-7 NIV

"Ask and it will be given to you; seek and you will find; knock and the door will be opened to you. For everyone who asks receives; the one who seeks finds; and to the one who knocks, the door will be opened."

—MATTHEW 7:7-8 NIV

Why is Prayer Important?

1. **Communication with God:** Prayer is a way to communicate directly with God. It involves speaking to Him, sharing your thoughts, feelings, and concerns, and listening for His guidance and

wisdom. It fosters a sense of closeness and intimacy with Him.

2. **Expression of Faith:** Prayer is an expression of faith and trust in God. It reflects a belief in His existence, love, and sovereignty over all things. We pray to acknowledge our dependence on God and His authority in our lives.

3. **Worship and Adoration:** Prayer is an act of worship and adoration. As believers, we offer prayers of praise and worship, acknowledging God's greatness, holiness, and glory. It is a way to honor and glorify Him.

4. **Confession and Forgiveness:** Through prayer, we confess our sins and seek God's forgiveness. We believe that God is merciful and just, and that sincere repentance leads to forgiveness and reconciliation with Him.

5. **Petition and Supplication:** We use prayer to make requests and seek God's intervention in various aspects of our lives. It includes praying for personal needs, the needs of others, guidance, healing, and provision.

6. **Thanksgiving:** Prayer is a means of expressing gratitude to God for His blessings, provisions, and

answered prayers. We are encouraged to have our hearts filled with thanksgiving.

7. **Seeking God's Will:** Prayer involves seeking and aligning with God's will. We pray for God's guidance and seek His plan and purpose for our lives.

8. **Intercession:** As believers, we engage in intercessory prayer, where we pray on behalf of others, including family, friends, and those in need or facing challenges. It is an act of love and compassion.

9. **Strength and Comfort:** In times of difficulty, prayer provides strength, comfort, and reassurance. We find solace in knowing that God is with us, cares for us, and provides peace in the midst of trials.

10. **Fellowship and Unity:** Prayer is often practiced in community settings, such as church gatherings, where believers come together to pray. It fosters fellowship, unity, and a sense of shared faith.

In summary, prayer is a sacred and meaningful practice that strengthens the believer's relationship with God, aligns us with His will, and provides spiritual nourishment, guidance, and comfort. It is an essential aspect of the Christian faith, emphasizing the intimate connection between the believer and the Heavenly Father through Jesus Christ.

In addition to strengthening our relationship with God, prayer also strengthens our hearts and our minds. This leads to the healing of your broken heart. Praying often will strengthen your spirit (spirit man or innermost being); which, in turn, strengthens you emotionally and spiritually.

PRAYING IN THE HOLY SPIRIT

Praying in the Holy Spirit is often referred to as "praying in tongues" or "speaking in tongues," a distinctive form of prayer guided by the Holy Spirit. It involves speaking or uttering words, sound, or languages not understood by the person praying or others present.

Tongues is a language that the Holy Spirit imparts to us as a gift, giving us the ability to communicate with God in a powerful way.

> *"For anyone who speaks in a tongue does not speak to people but to God. Indeed, no one understands them; they utter mysteries by the Spirit."*
> —I Corinthians 14:2 NIV

> *"But you, dear friends, by building yourselves up in your most holy faith and praying in the Holy Spirit . . ."*
> —Jude 1:20 NIV

Christians who pray in the Holy Spirit believe that the Holy Spirit is guiding their prayers and interceding on their behalf, often when they don't know how to pray effectively.

The Holy Spirit knows what we need, as well as what is the best solution for our situation (Romans 8:26-27). The Holy Spirit is able to plead for us in harmony with Father's will causing everything to work out for our good (Romans 8:28).

When you pray in tongues, you could possibly be prophesying good into your future or praying for protection for your loved ones without even knowing it. You can pray in tongues under your breath throughout the day. You can pray this powerful prayer while driving, while in the shower or when you are simply taking care of mundane tasks.

What is the Importance of Praying in the Holy Spirit?

1. **Spiritual Edification:** Praying or speaking in the Holy Spirit edifies or builds up the individual spiritually. It is a way to deepen your relationship with God and to experience a closer connection to the Holy Spirit.

2. **Praying in God's Will:** The Holy Spirit prays through the believer's spirit, ensuring that the prayers are aligned with God's will.

3. **Intercession:** Speaking in tongues can be used for intercession on behalf of others, allowing the Holy

Spirit to pray for others' specific needs or situations that the believer may not fully comprehend.

4. **Evidence of the Holy Spirit:** Speaking in tongues is evidence of the presence and the baptism of the Holy Spirit in a believer's life.

In summary, Jude 1:20-21 tells us that praying in tongues builds up our most holy faith. It builds you up spiritually and strengthens your faith. Praying in tongues strengthens your spirit man.

The Greek word for edifies means to restore, to rebuild, to repair. Praying in tongues brings divine healing and health to your body and mind, which results in a healed heart, a healed mind.

"Anyone who speaks in a tongue edifies themselves, but the one who prophesies edifies the church."
—I Corinthians 14:4 NIV

Principle 4

SPENDING QUALITY TIME WITH GOD

Spending quality time with God is an essential and highly valued practice. It involves setting aside dedicated moments for prayer, worship, Bible study, meditation, and reflection. The Christian belief system places a strong emphasis on nurturing a personal relationship with God through Jesus Christ, and spending quality time with God is a means to achieve and deepen that relationship.

The word "betimes" can only be found in the King James Version of the Bible. It means to earnestly seek God or seek Him early, which requires spending quiet, quality time with God.

"If thou wouldest seek unto God betimes, and make thy supplication to the Almighty;"

—Job 8:5 KJV

The following verse encourages believers to take time to be still and acknowledge the presence and sovereignty of God.

> *"Be still, and know that I am God; I will be exalted among the nations, I will be exalted in the earth."*
> —PSALM 46:10 NIV

Psalm 63:1-2 expresses the deep longing for God and the desire to seek Him earnestly (betimes).

> *"You, God, are my God, earnestly I seek you; I thirst for you, my whole being longs for you, in a dry and parched land where there is no water. I have seen you in the sanctuary and beheld your power and your glory."*
> —PSALM 63:1-2 NIV

Why is it Important to Spend Quality Time with God?

1. **Nurturing the Relationship:** God desires a personal relationship with each individual. Quality time with God allows you to nurture and strengthen that relationship by developing intimacy, trust, and a sense of closeness. The more quality time you spend with God, the more you will come to know Him and, in turn, you will be drawn closer to Him.

2. **Communication:** Just as communication is vital in any human relationship, it is also crucial in a

relationship with God. Spending time with God through prayer, conversation, and listening will help you express your thoughts, feelings, and concerns, and it allows you to hear from God. Spending time with God will help you to learn and recognize His voice.

3. **Worship and Adoration:** Quality time with God involves worship and adoration. We, as believers, believe that God is worthy of praise and honor, and spending time in worship is a way to acknowledge His greatness and express love and reverence.

4. **Studying the Word:** Bible study is an integral part of quality time with God. We believe that the Bible is God's inspired Word and studying it will help you understand His teachings, principles, and character.

5. **Seeking Guidance:** Time with God is an opportunity to seek His guidance and wisdom in making decisions when facing challenges and discerning His will for your life.

6. **Confession and Repentance:** Quality time with God includes confessing sins and seeking forgiveness. As Christians, we believe that

repentance and forgiveness are essential for maintaining a healthy relationship with God.

7. **Gratitude and Thanksgiving:** Christians express gratitude and thanksgiving to God for His blessings, provisions, and answered prayers during our time with Him.

8. **Holiness and Transformation:** Spending time with God helps in the process of becoming more Christ-like and living a life that reflects God's holiness and love.

9. **Peace and Joy:** It fosters a sense of peace, joy, and contentment by allowing you to cast your cares upon God and experience His presence.

In summary, spending quality time with God is essential for nurturing a personal relationship, seeking divine guidance, growing in faith, and experiencing the transformative power of God's presence. It is a deeply meaningful and spiritually enriching practice that allows believers to draw closer to their Heavenly Father through Jesus Christ.

As with the previous principles, spending quality time with God releases healing into your broken heart. Not only is it essential for fostering your personal relationship with God, but it's also essential for the healing process of your broken heart. When you are spending time with God, you are spending time with a healer.

Principle 5

PRAYING THE SCRIPTURES ALOUD

Praying the scriptures aloud is a powerful and meaningful practice. It involves reciting or speaking passages from the Bible in the form of prayers. This practice serves several important purposes and holds significance for those who are dealing with a broken heart.

> "... asking God, the glorious Father of our Lord Jesus Christ, to give you spiritual wisdom and insight so that you might grow in your knowledge of God. I pray that your hearts will be flooded with light so that you can understand the confident hope he has given to those he called—his holy people who are his rich and glorious inheritance.

I also pray that you will understand the incredible greatness of God's power for us who believe him. This is the same mighty power that raised Christ from the dead and seated him in the place of honor at God's right hand in the heavenly realms."

—EPHESIANS 1:17-20 NLT

"I ask God from the wealth of his glory to give you power through his Spirit to be strong in your inner selves, and I pray that Christ will make his home in your hearts through faith. I pray that you may have your roots and foundation in love, so that you, together with all God's people, may have the power to understand how broad and long, how high and deep, is Christ's love. Yes, may you come to know his love—although it can never be fully known—and so be completely filled with the very nature of God."

—EPHESIANS 3:16-19 GNT

What are the Benefits of Praying Scriptures Aloud?

1. **Strengthens You:** Praying the above-listed scriptures aloud will strengthen you through your spirit man to be able to get through losses and heartaches. This practice will help to heal your broken heart. The Word is alive and powerful (Hebrews 4:12).

2. **Reinforces Faith and Belief:** Praying scriptures aloud will reinforce your faith and belief in the truth and promises of God's Word. It allows you to

declare and affirm your trust in God's character and His promises.

3. **Helps You Stay on Track:** Although God hears your silent prayers, speaking your prayers aloud helps you to stay focused and reduces the likelihood of getting distracted by depression, heartache, loneliness, sadness, etc.

4. **Vocalization Reinforces Memory:** Praying scriptures aloud makes it easier for you to memorize the scriptures. As a result, you will know which scriptures to pray aloud when facing certain situations. For example, when you are dealing with a broken heart, you can pray aloud the afore-mentioned scriptures for healing and strengthening.

In summary, praying the scriptures aloud allows your heart to hear what you are saying. There's inherent power in what you speak and in the Word of God. This simple practice of praying the scriptures aloud will not only spiritually strengthen you, but it will strengthen your spiritual connection to God. This practice will also comfort you at those moments when your broken heart is hurting the most.

As you see, there are various benefits to praying the scriptures aloud. Especially, when you select scriptures that relate to your particular situation, as I have for dealing with a broken heart, as well as for strengthening. As I previously mentioned, the Word of God is alive and powerful!

Principle 6

PROTECTING YOUR EYES, EARS, AND HEART GATES

Protecting your eyes, ears, and heart gates underscores the importance of being vigilant and discerning about what you see, hear, and allow into your heart and mind. This practice emphasizes the need to guard against negative and ungodly influences when you are going through a period of healing your broken heart.

> *"Above all else, guard your heart, for everything you do flows from it."*
>
> —PROVERBS 4:23 NIV

> *"Finally, brothers and sisters, whatever is true, whatever is noble, whatever is right, whatever is pure, whatever is*

lovely, whatever is admirable—if anything is excellent or praiseworthy – think about such things."

—Philippians 4:8 NIV

"Do not conform to the pattern of this world, but be transformed by the renewing of your mind. Then you will be able to test and approve what God's will is – his good, pleasing and perfect will."

—Romans 12:2 NIV

What does Protecting Your Eyes, Ears, and Heart Gates Mean?

1. **Guarding Your Eyes:** Be mindful of what you expose yourself to visually, such things as images, media, and visual stimuli while you are healing. It means avoiding or filtering out content that might be triggers for you or content that is depressing or negative, as well as content that promotes sin, immorality, violence, or anything contrary to God's principles that would hinder the healing of your broken heart.

2. **Guarding Your Ears:** Be cautious about what you listen to including conversations, music, and messages. It means avoiding or limiting exposure to content that promotes negativity, gossip, slander, or ungodliness.

3. **Guarding Your Heart:** Your heart represents the core of your being, including your thoughts, emotions, and desires. In the Bible, heart and mind are often used interchangeably. What you allow to enter your eye and ear gates can impact your heart negatively or positively. Guarding your heart, your inner self, is being selective about what and/or who you allow to shape it.

Why it is Important?

1. **Maintaining Your Thoughts:** Protecting your eye, ear, and heart gates helps you maintain your thoughts by avoiding exposure to influences that can lead to further heartache.

2. **Protecting Your Thought Life:** As previously mentioned, what enters through your eyes and ears can affect your heart and mind (Proverbs 4:23). Guarding these gates ensures that your thoughts align with godly values, as well as help you to heal your brokenness.

3. **Resisting Negative Thoughts:** By protecting your eye and ear gates, you can resist certain thoughts and avoid falling into negative thinking that slows the progress of your heart and mind being healed (Philippians 4:8).

4. **Renewing Your Mind:** The Bible encourages the renewal of the mind with godly thoughts (Romans 12:2). Protecting your gates contributes to a positive and spiritually healthy thought life, which leads to a healed heart and mind.

In summary, as you go through your healing process, it's very important to be aware of what you allow your eyes and ears to entertain, as well as guard your heart not allowing any negative visual stimuli, information and/or thoughts to enter into your eye, ear, and heart gates, which can have a negative impact on your broken heart.

Principle 7

PARTAKE OF THE HOLY COMMUNION (FOR YOUR HEALING)

Communion, also known as the Lord's Supper or the Eucharist, is a sacred practice that involves the symbolic sharing of bread and wine (or grape juice) in remembrance of Jesus Christ's sacrifice on the cross. It is a significant ritual observed by Christians.

What is Communion?

1. **Symbolic Meal:** Communion is a symbolic meal that commemorates the Last Supper, which Jesus shared with His disciples on the night before His crucifixion.

2. **Elements:** Typically, unleavened bread (or crackers) and wine (or grape juice) are used as elements. The bread symbolizes Jesus' body, broken for believers, and the wine represents His blood, shed for the forgiveness of our sins.

3. **Remembrance:** Communion is a solemn act of remembering Jesus' sacrificial death, His atonement (covering our sins).

Benefits of Communion:

1. **Spiritual Renewal:** Communion can offer a sense of spiritual renewal, drawing believers closer to Christ as they reflect on His sacrifice and recommit themselves to Him.

2. **Emotional and Spiritual Healing:** We receive with faith everything Jesus died and paid for with His blood on the cross. In addition to forgiveness of our sins, He also died for our emotional and spiritual healing. Emotional healing is the healing of your broken heart and mind making you whole.

   Communion is a means of remembering Jesus' sacrifice when He was crucified in order for us to receive forgiveness and experience spiritual healing through Christ's atonement.

"But he was pierced for our rebellion, crushed for our sins. He was beaten so we could be whole. He was whipped so we could be healed."

—ISAIAH 53:5 NLT

"Bless and affectionately praise the Lord, O my soul, and do not forget any of His benefits; Who forgives all your sins, who heals all your disease;"

—PSALM 103:2-3 AMP

3. **Physical Healing:** Partaking (eating) Communion can be a means of seeking physical healing from ailments and illnesses. Eating the bread with faith, which is symbolic of Jesus' broken body as a result of being beaten and whipped, can heal you. He was whipped for our healing.

"Is anyone among you sick? Let them call the elders of the church to pray over them and anoint them with oil in the name of the Lord. And the prayer offered in faith will make the sick person well; the Lord will raise them up. If they have sinned, they will be forgiven."

—JAMES 5:14-15 NIV

4. **Connection to Jesus:** Partaking Communion on a regular basis will strengthen your connection to Jesus, as well as increase your faith in His ability to

heal your broken heart. Faith is the key to your healing, whether it's emotional, physical, or spiritual.

How to Partake the Holy Communion:

1. **Consecrate the Communion Elements:** Pray over your elements asking God to consecrate them setting them apart making them holy for your observation and remembrance of Jesus' sacrifice. Remember to partake the Communion with faith. Without faith, the Communion elements will just be ordinary.

2. **In a Worthy Manner:** When eating the bread, recognize it as a symbol of Jesus' broken body, which was broken for our healing and wholeness. When you eat the bread, focus on how Jesus received stripes for your healing in His body. We are not to treat the bread as an ordinary object, but to actually see Jesus receiving those stripes and being beaten beyond recognition as we eat the bread.

    When drinking the cup of grape juice or wine, discern it as a symbol of Jesus' blood He shed for forgiveness of your sins. When you drink the cup, envision Jesus' bleeding body as He hung on the cross for forgiveness of your sins and redeeming you from the curse of the law.

"So anyone who eats this bread or drinks this cup of the Lord unworthily is guilty of sinning against the body and blood of the Lord."
—1 Corinthians 11:27 NLT

3. **Honoring the Body of Christ:** Having a heartfelt gratitude for Jesus' sacrifice is a way to honor His body when you partake the holy Communion. We are to eat it with reverence for what Jesus did for us, and for how much He loves us.

   Another way to honor the body of Christ is to respect His fellow believers for whom Christ also died. In this sense, the body of Christ is the global church, other believers in Jesus Christ.

"For anyone who eats and drinks [without solemn reverence and heartfelt gratitude for the sacrifice of Christ], eats and drinks a judgment on himself if he does not recognize the body [of Christ]."
—I Corinthians 11:29 AMP

In summary, if you partake the holy Communion in a worthy manner, having a heartfelt gratitude for Jesus' sacrifice, and honoring the body of Christ, you will experience healing of your broken heart. Your relationship with Jesus will intensify. Your level of faith will increase, which is the key to your healing, whether it is emotional, physical, or spiritual.

Principle 8

PRAISING GOD IN ADVANCE FOR HEALING

P raising God in advance for healing is an approach to healing and well-being. It involves expressing gratitude and praise to God before experiencing the emotional or physical healing that you are seeking. Praising God during heartache will cause your broken heart to start healing.

> "Praise the Lord, my soul, and forget not all his benefits—
> who forgives all your sins and heals all your diseases."
> —PSALM 103:2-3 NIV

> "Therefore I tell you, whatever you ask for in prayer, believe
> that you have received it, and it will be yours."
> —MARK 11:24 NIV

"I will not die but live, and will proclaim what the Lord has done."

—Psalm 118:17 NIV

What Does Praising God in Advance for Healing Mean?

1. **Faith and Expectation:** Praising God in advance for healing is an expression of faith and expectation. It involves believing that God has the power and willingness to bring about healing and restoration in your life.

2. **Gratitude and Trust:** It's a way of demonstrating trust in God's goodness and sovereignty, even in the midst of illness or challenges. By praising in advance, you acknowledge God's ability to intervene.

3. **Confident Declaration:** It often involves making confident declarations or affirmations of healing, even before emotional or physical symptoms have completely subsided.

What is Praise?

Praise is the act of expressing reverence, adoration, and gratitude to God. It involves acknowledging and celebrating God's attributes, actions, and goodness. Praise can be expressed through prayer, song, worship, or a thankful heart.

Steps to Praising God in Advance for Healing:

1. **Faith and Belief:** Begin with a strong belief that God is capable of healing and that He desires the best for your well-being.

2. **Prayer and Thanksgiving:** Offer prayers of gratitude to God for His healing power and faithfulness. Thank Him for the healing you believe He will provide.

3. **Declaration:** Verbally declare your trust in God's healing power. Speak words of faith and assurance, declaring that you are healed in Jesus' name.

4. **Praise and Worship:** Engage in praise and worship as a way of magnifying God's greatness and goodness. Sing songs of hymns of praise that focus on His healing and restoration.

5. **Scripture Meditation:** Meditate on Bible verses that emphasize God's healing promises and His willingness to bring restoration.

Benefits of Praise:

1. **Deepened Faith:** Praise strengthens your faith and trust in God's ability to work miracles and bring about healing.

2. **Spiritual Connection:** It fosters a deeper connection with God and a sense of His presence.

3. **Peace and Comfort:** Praise can bring a sense of peace and comfort, even while in the midst of heartache.

4. **Positive Outlook:** It helps maintain a positive outlook and an attitude of gratitude.

5. **Encouragement:** Praise encourages and uplifts the spirit, providing hope and motivation.

In summary, praising God in advance for healing is a deep personal and faith-based practice. It's essential to approach it with a sincere heart and trust in God's will and timing, recognizing that His plans may not always align with our expectations. However, He expects us to yet believe in His promises of healing, whether it is emotional or physical, even when we don't know what His sovereign will is.

CONCLUSION

There are life experiences which bring joy, excitement, happiness, promotion and pleasure. On the other hand, there are life experiences filled with pain, tears, disappointment, rejection, and heart break. In times of heart break, seeing a clear path or direction is blurry.

Those of you who have experienced domestic violence, infidelity, and/or loss of a loved one embracing these eight principles will position your heart and mind to heal going from brokenness to wholeness! You can truly experience the joy and peace Jesus died for you to have in your heart, mind, and spirit.

Remember the number eight represents new beginnings. Applying these eight principles will help not only to heal your broken heart but to embrace your new life: Your new beginnings!

ACKNOWLEDGMENTS

Thanks to Apostle K. C. Sparks whose prophecy inspired me to write this book.

Thanks to my Pastor, Apostle Dr. Earl l. Newton, Sr. Pastor of Life Changers Global Ministries, whose teaching and leadership have inspired me to excellence.

ABOUT THE AUTHOR

RITA J. CARTWRIGHT

This memoir is an account of Rita J. Cartwright's life from the age of sixteen years old until now. From the age of sixteen to the present, Rita has experienced many up close and personal brokenhearted moments. Because of her experience, she is an expert on the topic of **"How to Heal Your Broken Heart."** She was inspired by a prophecy from a prophet saying: *"She is to write a book to help women with broken hearts heal."* From the leading of the prophet, this book was birth. Her desire is for brokenhearted women to be healed.

Five years ago, Rita launched a nonprofit organization called *Go Beyond the Limit* (GBTL) as a way to give back to her community. GBTL is organized to provide online training for survivors of domestic violence on how to become online entrepreneurs. Go here for more information on Go Beyond the Limit's training program: https://gobeyondthelimit.org.

She earned a Bachelor of Science degree in marketing at the age of forty-five from Arizona State University (ASU). In addition to earning an undergraduate degree, Rita is an entrepreneur and owner of RJ's Digital Solutions, LLC. Go here for more information on her digital marketing business: https://rjsdigitalsolutions.com.

Rita currently resides in Phoenix, Arizona. She is a mother, grandmother, and a great-grandmother. In addition, Rita is a devout believer in the Godhead of Glory. She also volunteers at her church as the Director of the Media and Bereavement Ministries.

BIBLIOGRAPHY

BIBLE REFERENCES

https://www.biblegateway.com/versions/
Amplified-Bible-Classic-Edition-AMPC/

https://www.biblegateway.com/versions/
New-Living-Translation-NLT-Bible/

https://www.biblegateway.com/versions/Amplified-Bible-AMP/

https://www.biblegateway.com/versions/
English-Standard-Version-ESV-Bible/

The New International Version (NIV) Bible - Search and Read
Online (biblestudytools.com)

AMPC Bible | Amplified Bible, Classic Edition | YouVersion

www.ingramcontent.com/pod-product-compliance
Lightning Source LLC
Chambersburg PA
CBHW051540120626
46551CB00013B/1304